HOW TO
RALLY

HOW TO
RALLY

WISDOM
from a
LIFE SPENT
BEATING THE ODDS

RICHARD ADER

Forefront
BOOKS

How To Rally
Wisdom from a Life Spent Beating the Odds

Copyright © 2021 Richard Ader

All Rights Reserved.

Published by Forefront Books.

Cover Design by Bruce Gore, Gore Studio Inc.
Interior Design by Bill Kersey, KerseyGraphics

ISBN: 978-1-63763-029-7
ISBN: 978-1-63763-030-3 (eBook)

DEDICATION

———

To Pam. I met you in May, we were engaged in September, and married in January. More than 56 years later, every day is better than the one before. You have supported me through the events in this book as my doctor, my nurse, my trainer, and, of course, my love. You have been my everything, and I love you very much.

CONTENTS

ACKNOWLEDGMENTS. *9*

FOREWORD. *13*

INTRODUCTION *17*

LESSON ONE *27*
    Compete Against Others, Compete Against Yourself

LESSON TWO. *45*
    Be Strategic and Understand the Importance of Risk

LESSON THREE *69*
    When You Hit an Obstacle, Figure Out a Way Past It

LESSON FOUR *83*

Loyalty and Compassion Are the Keys to Lasting Relationships

LESSON FIVE *99*

Live with Honesty and Integrity

LESSON SIX *109*

Set Goal after Goal after Goal

LESSON SEVEN................................. *121*

Give Back, Whenever You Can

LESSON EIGHT................................. *135*

You're Never Too Young, and You're Never Too Old

ACKNOWLEDGMENTS

First, of course, thank you to my wife, Pam. I dedicated this book to you and feel so lucky to wake up next to you every morning. To my children and grandchildren, your support throughout my crises and my recovery has bolstered my spirits and kept me going. I look forward to every moment spent with each of you.

To my sister, Sylvia, thank you for a lifetime of friendship. To my mother, my hero, I wish you'd had a chance to read this.

To Ronny, what can I say about a best friend that hasn't been said before? You know what you mean to me.

To my physicians, Dr. Evelyn Horn, Dr. Erica Jones, and Dr. George Thomas, you saved my life, and I am deeply indebted. To my nurses, Mike, Pete, Chris, Eric, and Joe, your hard work with me on the healing process is something I am truly thankful for. To my trainers, Stacy, Larry, and Eric, you have helped me build up my body and build back my strength. The skills and dedication of all of you fill me with gratitude.

To David Ledy, David Silvers, Jack Genende, and David Grazioli, thank you for all that you do to keep the business running, and for all your help and support. Thank you to Barbara Gunzberg, who protects me and watches out for me always.

To Jeremy Blachman, your help and assistance on this project has been invaluable. Without you, this book would be a paragraph long.

To Patrick McEnroe, thank you for the foreword, and for your friendship and partnership over the years. To Billie Jean King, thank you for letting me share our story, and to Rusty Kanokogi, I think of you and miss your presence constantly.

Finally, to Jonathan Merkh and the entire team at Forefront Books, thank you for bringing my words to life and making this book a reality.

FOREWORD

By Patrick McEnroe

———————

I was lucky enough to have an incredible father, and I'm lucky enough to still have two great older brothers. Throughout my life, I have been lucky to have had many mentors as well, both in tennis and in life.

But I can honestly say that, for me, the only person who has encompassed all of those qualities in one is Richard Ader.

I have known Richard for almost twenty-five years. We met through tennis, as I've met many of my friends throughout my fifty-two years involved in the game (I'm now fifty-five years young).

Richard has always been a person I could talk to . . . about my life, my family, and my career. We worked as partners in a business venture called World Team Tennis, the co-ed tennis league started by the legendary Billie Jean King over forty years ago. We did the work not because we could make a lot of money (we could have lost some), but because we loved the game.

Working together throughout the World Team Tennis years, Richard taught me so much about business, and, even more, about how to treat people in business and in life.

I knew that Richard was very successful in his real estate business, but he was always more interested in discussing my life, my story, and my goals. We would meet often at his favorite Midtown Manhattan restaurant, down the street from his office. He would always be early, sitting at his customary table, waiting for his tennis buddy.

I looked forward to those lunches because I knew I could always get the straight story from Richard. His pearls of wisdom stayed with me as I navigated my way through my post-tennis-playing career.

Richard became one of my most trusted confidants. I have come to see him as a father figure, an older brother figure, a mentor figure, and, honestly, over the years, as a true, true friend.

Reading Richard's story is just incredible. I knew some of it: his basketball playing days; his upbringing; his awesome wife, Pam; his family (he's the proudest father and grandfather there is); and his tremendously successful real estate business. But I didn't know it all.

I have been lucky enough to meet many of Richard's friends and family through the years at his U.S. Open suite, where Richard holds court in his chair, taking in the tennis all day and night.

Recently, I was able to hit tennis balls with Richard again. To see his dedication to get back on the court after all he has been through is an absolute inspiration.

Thank you, Richard, for being you. And I love your new two-handed backhand. We should have switched to it years ago.

INTRODUCTION

I was looking straight at death. But I refused to let it take me.

It was March 2019, and I was in the recovery room after an ablation procedure on my heart. My doctor told me that it was a success. But the next thing I remember, it was two days later, and I woke up thinking I was dead. I'm told that my heart stopped and all my organs began failing. I had been put into a medically induced coma. My family was told to prepare for my demise. They thought it was the end. My doctors thought it was the end. Everyone thought it was the end.

But it wasn't the end.

In many ways, it turned out to be just the beginning. After almost two months in the hospital, after losing more than twenty pounds and virtually all of my muscle mass, I was unable to stand on my own. In fact, I was unable to do much of anything. My doctors told me I might never walk again, and certainly that I'd never again play tennis, the sport I'd loved for decades.

To me, there had to be a path forward. There always is. Finding that path, no matter the odds, is what has driven me my entire life. Professionally, I became a pioneer in the field of net lease real estate, building a career of more than fifty years finding ever-greater ways to benefit my clients, even as laws and regulations changed. In that work, I have needed a careful, reasoned understanding of risk and reward. I've had to set bold-but-realistic goals, take decisive action, and invest time and energy with an eye toward the future. The skills that have served me well in real estate are remarkably similar to those that have been needed for a successful recovery. That's how this book emerged.

That's how I believe my story can help *you*, no matter where you are in your recovery, and what you're hoping to achieve.

It was during a tennis match with a friend that the events unfolded that ultimately led to this book. I was playing tennis on Randall's Island in New York. I remember walking to one side of the court and then falling to the ground, landing smack on my face. Luckily, it was right next to a training location for the New York City Fire Department, and there were six EMTs eating breakfast just a few hundred feet away. They revived me and insisted that I go to the hospital. But this wasn't a sports injury. I fell because my heart was out of rhythm, a condition known as atrial fibrillation, and my heart was out of rhythm because it was beginning to fail.

My father died of a heart attack at age fifty-three, when I was just a teenager. Back then, doctors didn't know there was much you could do to fix a weak heart. My father had three heart attacks, yet no one ever told him to go a gym and take care of himself. He went to work, came home, drank a glass of whiskey, and smoked a cigar. Generations of people with weak hearts simply died earlier than they otherwise might have because the knowledge wasn't there, the medicine wasn't there, and the equipment wasn't there. I was much luckier. The doctors saw that I had a weak heart, and they began to intervene. After the Randall's Island incident, my doctors installed a defibrillator, a device that can shock your heart back into its correct rhythm.

But that was just the start of my struggles.

Not long after, doctors also found that I had a leaky valve. There was a choice between open heart surgery and a less invasive procedure that would clip the valve using a tiny tube. Doctors examined me, interviewed me, and tried to figure out the best path forward. Fortunately, I qualified for the clip, and it was a successful procedure.

But I still wasn't done.

In some ways, my body responded *too* well to the cardiac medications they gave me. I had drugs to regulate my blood pressure, but the pressure kept falling too low, so I felt dizzy and lightheaded. One day, playing tennis again, I started to feel faint. I sat down on the court to avoid another fall, and then I was taken to the hospital where they found it necessary to give my heart another shock. My doctors wanted me to have a procedure called an *ablation*, where small areas of heart tissue are treated in order to restore the normal heartbeat. As it turned out, that was just one of a few ablations I would need. After the last one, in March 2019, I was back in my room when the doctor told me that it all went well. That's the last thing I remember before the world turned black.

Lights were flashing outside my door, bells were ringing, and doctors and nurses stormed into my room to save me. (My family tells this story better than I can.)

My pulse was 190, and my heart was in overdrive. I was dying. Every vital sign was down to zero, so I was placed on a ventilator and put into a medically induced coma. For two days, no one knew if I would ever wake up or what my condition would be if I did. I had dreams while I was in the coma, or semi-dreams, I suppose, where I was listening to the television in my room and hearing the sounds of life around me, but I couldn't respond. Suddenly, there was a dog by my side, and it was *my* dog, Oliver. We both saw death, right in front of us. Oliver's eyes flew open and that forced me to open mine. Suddenly, I was awake.

There I was, in the hospital bed, my family surrounding me. I thought I was dead. I kept asking for proof that I was alive. I saw Notre Dame Cathedral in flames on the television screen, and thought that couldn't be real. For almost two months I was in the hospital. They were keeping my heart beating artificially at first with a balloon pump attached to my leg. I was completely incapacitated, unable to move, unable to do anything without serious assistance.

After that event, I drove myself to a remarkable recovery. I was playing tennis again, and I was back at work in my office. But my heart was still functioning poorly. My doctors installed a machine called a CardioMEMS to measure the fluid on my lungs, in order to make sure it wasn't building up from the heart failure. To use this machine, I had to lie on a special pillow that could take the necessary readings, and then transmit those readings to my doctor so he could monitor my lung function. I had to do this every single day.

In September 2020, I experienced a second monumental crisis. I was back in the hospital for a cardiac catheterization procedure to examine how my heart was working, and it showed that my cardiac output was very low. In the presence of the doctors, my heart went crazy. It was way out of rhythm and not working right. The defibrillator was doing its job, trying to shock my heart back into rhythm, and the power of the shocks actually knocked me over. I was told there wasn't much of a chance I would survive many more of those kinds of attacks. I was getting close to the end. They even suggested that my wife should alert our children!

The doctors told me I needed to reconsider an option they had shown me before, a Left Ventricular Assist Device (known as an LVAD), a battery-operated mechanical heart pump that might now be the only way to keep me alive. When I had previously been shown the device, I was told it would potentially increase my lifespan but at that point it hadn't yet become a necessity. I was still hoping I could survive without it. An LVAD becomes a seriously life-altering machine: a person has to wear a battery pack and can't be submerged in water or take a normal shower. It limits you in many ways. Frankly, I was not comfortable at all having a machine like that put into my body. No way, no chance. Until there was no way and no chance to survive without it.

I wanted to live, after all. There in the hospital, being told I would not survive without the LVAD, I emotionally told Pam I wasn't ready to die. I finally agreed to the procedure. I would have to start my recovery all over again.

There are lessons here about persistence and attitude even in the face of repeated hardships, having to retrace your steps, and wondering if all of the effort you've put into something has been for naught. I never planned on writing a book. But as I embarked on my recovery with the help of wonderful nurses, trainers, and caregivers, the doctors simply couldn't believe my progress. They were truly astonished to watch videos I sent to them of me back on a tennis court, hitting the ball, and doing things they had never seen another LVAD patient even attempt. People surrounding me begged me to share my story, insisting that the principles that have driven me in my life would apply to many others who were looking for inspiration.

It is my firm conviction that we can all train ourselves to get through anything by thinking strategically, by setting goals, and by using competition as the driving force in our lives. If this book can help just a few readers find the inner strength to recover, to harness their willpower in pursuit of a goal, and to not just get back to the life they once lived, but to embark on a new, different, and better life, then writing it will have been more than worth it.

You can be as weak as a person can be, debilitated and completely reliant on help. You can be in a terrible place, physically or mentally, and still work your way back, if you have the right mindset. If I could do it, in my late 70s, after a crisis as serious as mine, you can do it too. In these pages that follow, I hope to teach you "how to rally."

LESSON ONE

Compete Against Others,
Compete Against Yourself

The first lesson I want to share is about competition because in many ways, I think competition is the key to everything. Whether you're competing against others or against yourself, you always need to try to push past limits and achieve new goals. There are people who don't want to know how others are doing, and who don't want the pressure of trying to win at anything, but I've never been that way. I want to know how my progress compares to other patients because in my mind, they're my competition. I want every member of my team to understand that I will do more than the average person, and that I desperately want to be pushed. That's the attitude you need to foster within yourself to make the most of your recovery. You must build a team to support you, and you must rely on that team.

The book *Jonathan Livingston Seagull* was published in 1970 when I was a young professional first rising up the ranks; it went on to sell over a million copies. It tells the story of a seagull who wanted to be the best damn seagull ever. Flying for him wasn't just about finding food, it was about soaring. It was about how we all could be so much more than society conditions us to believe, so much more than we ever imagine. Like that seagull, I was ambitious and hungry. I wanted to be the best and had the confidence that I could succeed at anything I set my mind to. That ambition has driven me throughout my life, and it's a must-have ingredient for achievement, no matter what it is you're aiming for.

The truth is, my love for competition started early. There was never a time in my life when I wasn't playing a sport. (Or if I was not playing, then I was watching. My wife says I will watch anything on television that has a ball, ping pong included.) Before there was tennis, which I didn't take up until I was in my 30s, there was baseball, and then there was basketball. For many years, basketball was my life. Being a star on my high school basketball team helped me get to college by earning a full basketball scholarship to the University of Vermont. My college career was a storied one for UVM, eventually landing me in the school's athletic hall of fame. In a three-year varsity career, I started almost every game, averaging 10.8 points. I was named to all-conference and all-state teams, and as a junior I once scored twenty-three points in a game against our rivals, the University of Massachusetts. That was a real feat in those days; there was no three-point shot back then and no shot clock, meaning that it wasn't unusual for players to just hold onto the ball, keeping scoring way down.

It was tremendous how sports brought out an intensity in me, a competitive spirit both physically and mentally. The workouts excited me and so did the strategy of the game. Once I moved into the real world, I missed that, and I never thought I'd be able to recapture it. But in my thirties, I stumbled upon tennis and realized that individual sports could fill that void in a way I hadn't imagined possible.

My hunger for competition was why I switched to tennis initially. There was a former college tennis player with whom I came into contact through work, and he was very good. He didn't realize it, but he was my motivation. My sights were set on beating him. It didn't hurt that I'd noticed great tennis players always seemed to look younger and be in great shape for their age. It also didn't hurt that the footwork in tennis is surprisingly similar to basketball. Those skills carried over, and I became very good, very quickly. But the lessons were different from the ones I learned playing team sports.

When playing an individual sport, you need an incredible amount of range, at least when you're playing singles. There are no teammates to rely upon to help you cover any skills where you are weak. You need to learn everything that's required in the game. You might have great strokes, but if you can't control where you're hitting the ball, you'll lose. If you can only play well against people who hit the ball back hard, and you have trouble with softer returns, you'll lose too. You need to learn how to adjust to beat all kinds of players, and how to be strong even after you lose a point.

The mental part of a game such as tennis is huge. It's all about resilience and the ability to admit your own shortcomings. In basketball, you can blame others. *If only my teammate had made the basket*, you might think, or, *if only they'd passed to me a second earlier, things might have turned out differently.* In tennis, you can only blame yourself.

Eventually I reached my goal and was able to beat the colleague who didn't even know I was chasing him. But reaching that goal just meant setting another, and before too long, I was a member of the United States tennis team competing in the Maccabiah Games in Israel. The Maccabiah Games are often referred to as the Jewish Olympics, with 10,000 athletes from 85 participating countries around the world competing every four years in more than two dozen sports. Past competitors have included Olympic swimmer Mark Spitz, Olympic gymnast Kerri Strug, 1950s basketball star Dolph Schayes, and many more. Like the Olympics, the Maccabiah Games start with a flag ceremony as uniformed players carry their countries' flags through a ceremony full of fanfare. Participating on behalf of my country was an incredible, humbling experience.

The first time I competed was in 1981. I was overwhelmed. I was a real estate guy from New York, not a professional tennis player on the tour. Competitors needed to arrive in Israel two weeks before the Games started, and we were practicing every day, serving and hitting. I started tearing the muscles in my shoulder; it was so much more practice than my arm was used to. But to compete, it was worth it. I learned through the intensity of the workouts and the intensity of the competition on the court that world-level tournament play was very different from what I was accustomed to as an amateur.

Four years later, in 1985, I went back to the Games, and I won a bronze medal playing doubles with a friend of mine. That friend went on to win the silver medal in the singles competition. I was accepted to the team in 1989 but I was unable to go because of commitments at work; I went again in 1993 and this time I won a silver medal. These were experiences of a lifetime, and these memories have stayed with me. But what I learned most of all was that with hard work, I could compete at the international level, and my combination of resilience and mental strength was enough to outlast some of my more physically gifted opponents.

Playing both team sports and individual sports over the course of my life has made me understand that to succeed, and to recover, you need two important but very different kinds of skills: You need to master everything it takes to win as a team, and you also need to do everything possible to be a strong individual. That maps perfectly to what happens in recovery. You do have a team, and you need to work with that team, but in many ways, you are also entirely on your own. There are lessons for all aspects of life to take from team sports and from individual pursuits.

Let's start with teams. Even all these decades later, I still see basketball as such an amazing game. It requires both physical skills and strategy, footwork and focus, and the ability to work together with your teammates. When I was playing ball, I studied the professionals. I would watch what they were doing and try to copy them. It helped me get into their heads and understand the game from their perspectives. I had the drive to succeed from the start, but what I found in basketball is that my own drive wasn't enough. I could be great, but I also had to surround myself with the right kind of greatness in others. That's the team lesson: your own drive isn't always enough if you don't have the right support.

I had an insight a long time ago that a lot of people have realized in the years since. The best teams aren't necessarily the ones that are filled with all-stars. The very best teams, able to win consistently and go on championship runs, realize that players each need different skills. The legendary Boston Celtics coach and executive Red Auerbach taught this to the basketball world, and it's been replicated again and again. One player might be a great inside shooter, another might be the rebound guy, and a third might be the playmaker. If they're all trying to do everything, even if they're hugely talented on their own, they will inevitably get in one another's way. Everyone's desire to do everything will cause conflict, and the team will fail.

This certainly translates exceptionally well to the business world. I built my real estate business understanding that it was critical to cover all of the disciplines, and let people own their own domains. They needed to be the experts and to feel like they could grow and lead. This means two things: hire diversely and give everyone a role they can fully own. In my firm, someone needed to service clients, someone needed to do the accounting, and someone had to worry about the legal side. We needed people to make the deals but also people to handle the ongoing business once the deals were done. So I needed to hire for all of these different disciplines. If you're missing a single skill, even at the lowest rung, something will inevitably go wrong. You have to set your business up so that doesn't happen.

At the same time, you can't have two people jostling for the same role. The better the people, the more important it is to make sure they each have separate strengths. Everyone who succeeds in business is competitive even if they're hiding it. It is almost a universal rule that successful people *have* to be competitive. Of course, competitive people have egos, which can be channeled effectively to drive good work, but egos can also get in the way if people are jealous of their colleagues. If your people want one another's jobs, performance will suffer. If they're threatened by another's success, or worried about their compensation, performance will suffer. The culture will suffer as well. But if the legal expert has no interest in being a salesman, and the salesman doesn't want to service accounts, and the account team knows that others are supporting their efforts, then everyone can work together *as a team*. The easiest way for an organization to thrive is to find a way to avoid office politics. There doesn't need to be drama.

Without the drama that weighs down some organizations, with stars able to excel across the company and driven to be great, there is no limit to what you can achieve. And there shouldn't be any limits to your aspirations. If you aim for mediocrity, that's what you'll get. But if you aim for perfection, you'll reach the sky. (There's that seagull again.)

This all translates to recovery. You need the right team around you, people with all of the different skills and talents to help you regain more and more of your health, and your mental and physical functions. That means doctors, of course, but it also means physical therapists, nurses, and the emotional support of friends and family. It's just like in business: everyone on your team needs to understand each person's expertise and let them do their jobs. You should be informed about all of it, but you should have people you trust so that you're not second-guessing every exercise your trainer tells you do.

You know your own body and your own mind better than anyone, of course. You also know your goals and what you want to achieve. But you can't do it all yourself. If you pick the right experts for each role, they can add so much value beyond what you'd ever imagine. I've worked with several trainers during my recovery. I have three trainers as I'm writing this book, and I probably push them just as hard as they push me because I can see the difference it makes.

It's important to measure your improvement, study it, and make sure you're continuously making progress. If you stagnate, make changes. A good trainer will get you beyond where you think you can go and will take you further and further. When you start to achieve beyond what you perceive as your limit, it's a huge boost mentally. It gives you the confidence to think you can do even more, and it gives your team the encouragement to keep thinking of new things for you to accomplish.

I show my doctors videos of my recovery because I want their praise, and I want their feedback and support. But mostly I want them to know that I'm not kidding around. I need them to understand how serious I am about my recovery, serious about getting back function, and serious about holding them accountable for how they contribute to my success.

Then there's the individual side of things. There may be people around you filling all kinds of different roles, but you still need to take ownership and master your part. You also need to develop the mental toughness to stay focused even in the highest-stakes situation. You need to excel even when there's no one to rely on but yourself. You need to defer to workmates who excel in different disciplines or bring different skills to the table, just as you would on a basketball team. You also need to see and understand the whole picture and take ownership not just for your performance but also for the ultimate result, just as you would in a game of tennis. You need to be able to learn whatever is necessary to succeed, even if it pushes you beyond your core capabilities and out of your comfort zone. You need to be able to compete at the highest level and find a way to win.

This is all so relevant to recovery. You are the one who will or won't reach your goals. No matter the contributions of everyone around you, it's your actions, your motivation, and your willingness to work that will ultimately be all that matter. You have to live with the results, and either end up with a life you're happy with or disappointed by your limitations. Your doctor may very well care about your recovery, hopefully quite deeply, and your trainers may be rooting for you and trying their best, but they always get to move on to the next patient. You don't get that same luxury. Your family and friends may be supporting you and helping you in whatever ways they can, but if you don't put in the work, push yourself every day, and stay focused on your goals, you won't get better.

Eighteen months after the March 2019 incident, when I had been placed in the medically induced coma, I was back up to 75 percent of my old capacity. I was feeling strong and feeling healthy. But then I had the other setback and was back to square one. I could have given up. I could have said, *I've competed enough, and it is time to rest*. But competitors don't stop competing, and winners don't let themselves rest. The reality is that recovery never stops, just like work on anything that's important can never stop. Athletes practice year-round, not just during their sport's season. Successful people can't let up. The competitive spirit kept me going, kept me fighting, and kept me trying to be my best.

Sports was great training for my recovery because sports taught me that you can always improve, always get better, and always put yourself in the best position to have a chance to win. No one in my family was athletic, but I dedicated myself to physical training and to keeping my body in shape. I believe it's largely because of how physically fit I was prior to my heart troubles that I have been able to recover as well as I have, but no matter where you start from, you need to remember that you have the power to shape yourself into the person you aspire to be.

That's *not* to say it's easy. We all see athletes on television who are carried off the field or the court, and then they pop back on your screen within weeks. My ability to pop back up from a setback is a little different, affected by my age, of course. You do inevitably slow down as you get older. But you can absolutely overcome your age and still keep improving and getting stronger, no matter what.

That power to improve comes from always trying to compete, always seeing victory as possible, and always pushing yourself to be your best. It's the lesson I wanted to start out with, because I think it's been so critical to my recovery. But it's not the only lesson I want to share, and it's not the only reason that I've found the ability to build myself back.

You can be as competitive as you want, but you must also learn several skills that will manage your competitive spirit and give you the ability to stay strong, and the mindset to find a way past obstacles, traps, and the allure of bad choices. The next lesson is about strategic thinking and understanding risk, a topic that can't be overemphasized, whether in business, in life, or in recovery.

LESSON TWO

*Be Strategic and Understand
the Importance of Risk*

Let me start this lesson with a story about my childhood. Growing up, my father was a successful businessman. He owned an electrical supply store, and, from an economic perspective, our family was comfortable. We lived in a Manhattan apartment and even had a country house an hour north of the city in Peekskill, New York. And then, unexpectedly, at least to me and my sister, our world came crashing down.

First, the store. The electrical supply business in the city had been concentrated in one neighborhood, East Harlem, and my father was right in the center of it. But the area was growing rougher in the 1950s, and some of his competitors were beginning to move. Stores were relocating, and pretty soon his store was the only one left. "I'll be the last man standing," he decided, but once he was the only one there, it wasn't worth it to customers to make the trip. Buyers were accustomed to getting all their needs met in one area of the city, and they stopped coming. It didn't take long for him to go bankrupt, and going bankrupt was a huge embarrassment.

In the wake of my father's business failing, his health failed as well. I remember my bar mitzvah, when I turned thirteen years old. The week of the event, my father had his second heart attack. He refused to go to the hospital. Doctors brought an oxygen tent into our apartment. He made it to the bar mitzvah but his health declined precipitously from then on. He opened a new store, on 1st Avenue, but it wasn't the same. It was fifty steps down for him in terms of prestige and money. As far as I could tell, the shame and embarrassment from his business failure overwhelmed him, contributing to his ultimate fate. Two years after my bar mitzvah, he had another heart attack and died. I was fifteen years old.

We didn't know until after he passed away that his life insurance policy had lapsed due to a failure to pay the premiums. That experience shaped me. Parents don't generally discuss the household finances with the children, and certainly they didn't back then, so my sister and I had no idea that we had been living so close to the edge. We didn't understand what it meant to suddenly not be able to afford our apartment, our private school, or anything. My mother had done some interior decorating work, but she couldn't bring in nearly enough money to pay our rent. We had to move to a smaller, less expensive apartment, and I still don't know how she managed to pay the bills. She tried to take over my father's electrical supply business, but in those days, women didn't run businesses like those, and she was subjected to a tremendous amount of abuse.

My father had told her not to worry about money because she had good kids who would take care of her. Unfortunately, he died so young, before we were established enough in our lives and careers to be of much help. The combined Social Security checks that arrived each month were barely enough to sustain us. My mother certainly became my hero. It's amazing that she was able to do as much as she did, honestly. She opened a store and designed a lamp that even brought her small royalty checks until the day she died. She did her best, but it was still so hard.

We adjusted to the situation and its impact on our young lives; we knew we needed to find a way to move forward without adding to our mother's stress. My sister, Sylvia, was (and is) brilliant. She graduated from high school at age 14, and absolutely could have had her choice of Ivy League colleges if her age hadn't been a factor. But there was also no money. She graduated from Hunter College and ended up working in the magazine industry, at *Mademoiselle* and *McCall's*. She sent our mother some of her salary to help keep her going.

My private school tuition became impossible to pay. I will always be grateful for the scholarship that the McBurney School offered me in order to remain in high school there and graduate with my friends. Even so, I was certainly envious of my classmates. Over the school holidays, they would go to Florida or on other trips, but I would just be at home. One of my friends had parents who were very generous, always inviting me over to their apartment and treating me well. Although I was and still am very appreciative, mostly it just reminded me of all that I had lost.

I realized as a high school kid on scholarship that for me to go to college, financial help would be critical. My best and only hope was a basketball scholarship. I knew that I needed to push myself to my maximum capability in order to convince colleges to take a chance on me. It was not easy. A number of schools told me they hadn't had good luck with New York City players and wouldn't even consider me. Smaller schools were easier to approach, and more open to the possibility. Two friends of mine were already playing on the University of Vermont team and urged the coach to give me a chance. There's a lesson there about treating everyone whose paths you cross with the respect and kindness they deserve (and it's a lesson that will show up again later in this book). You never know how people might play a role in your future, and how unexpected kindnesses can emerge.

The University of Vermont coach offered me the scholarship on a trial basis for one semester. I worked my hardest and became one of the highest scorers on the team, earning the scholarship for the rest of my time at the university. Two years later, I justified the coach's faith in me by making the all-conference team.

Still, life on scholarship was not easy. The coach of my freshman basketball team was also the varsity baseball coach. He sought me out at practice one day and asked me to come out for the varsity baseball team. It would have been a wonderful opportunity, and I would have loved it, but I actually couldn't afford to buy a baseball glove. I had to turn him down.

My scholarship covered the educational part of my expenses at Vermont but I still had to earn every penny that I spent on food. I worked as a waiter in the student café at first, and later worked as a waiter in my fraternity house to earn my meals. That was an uncomfortable situation, having to play the role of waiter to my friends. Out of the blue, I got a call one day from the Merchant's Bank of Burlington. An officer there wanted to speak to me. In appreciation for my efforts playing basketball for the school, he wanted to offer me a grant to cover my food expenses. It was quite a break, but I didn't always get a break.

For instance, my Spanish teacher informed us during our first class that any more than three missed sessions would mean automatic failure. Failing a class would put my scholarship in jeopardy since I needed to achieve a certain grade point average. After that class, I told the teacher that I was on the basketball team, and on scholarship, and that away games might force me to miss more than three sessions through no fault of my own. She couldn't have cared less, and said she would fail me if that happened, no exception. Sure enough, when the schedule forced travel that took me out of class, she really did give me an F in Spanish.

I ended up having to go to my coach and tell him that my scholarship was in jeopardy. He needed to give me an A in physical education or I'd lose the scholarship. When I was home over the summer break, I fulfilled the language requirement at summer school, but I have to admit that none of it stuck. I may have passed Spanish class, but please don't ask me to say anything more complicated than *"Hola!"*

My experience going from a comfortable financial existence to being on the edge at age fifteen, and then having
to work my way through school, showed me that money
doesn't make you a different person, and certainly not
a better person. I saw the ways that some of my classmates disrespected the waitstaff, and those impressions
stuck with me. It taught me to understand that there
is value in everyone's role and everyone's contribution.
That feels more relevant than ever as I go through my
recovery. I feel so grateful for the nurses, trainers, and
caregivers who have helped me, and I try my very best
to express that appreciation and treat them like family.
They have gifts and abilities that I don't, and their roles
are so critical to so many people.

But the larger lesson for this chapter is another idea
that emerges from the story of my youth: losing everything as a teenager gave me an acute perspective on
risk. I entered adulthood understanding that nothing is

guaranteed and that you have to approach every decision you make with the realization that things might not work out. You need to have safeguards in place to make sure you don't wind up in the same position as my family did. You need to appreciate the importance of security, of guarantees, and of careful, mindful decision-making.

I've tried my best to live a life of carefully managed risk. My first job out of college was at what was then called the Chemical Corn Exchange Bank (it later became Chemical Bank, and then merged with Chase in 1996 to eventually become part of JPMorgan Chase). I was so naive in terms of understanding the corporate world that I didn't even know to wear a suit to the interview; I ended up having to borrow one from a friend.

Back then, I imagined I'd be at that first job forever. After all, they had a great retirement plan. My friend Ronny jokes that no other 22-year-old would have been thinking about pensions and retirement at that point in his life, but it's true. Security was so important to me. For years, starting a business felt like something far too risky for me to pursue. I was fully prepared to sacrifice greater upside for downside protection. My needs were never overwhelming as I'm a homebody at heart, and I never looked to live an extravagant life. Preventing financial disaster was worth everything.

Ultimately, things didn't turn out as simple as that. Chemical Bank didn't end up being my first and last employer. But at every turn, moves were made with exceptional care, knowing that things in the real world can absolutely fail. In real estate, there are many ways to take on risk, but I've always managed my business with the goal of protecting the money I'm entrusted with, even if that sometimes means missing out on opportunities that in hindsight would have been good transactions.

There will be time to explain how these same principles apply in recovery, but I first wanted to talk a bit about strategic thinking, in work and in life, and about how to approach the decisions you make. There was a lot to learn at Chemical Bank. The head of my first branch assignment was a former priest, and he passed along a lesson that has always stuck with me: as you go through life, put yourself in the other person's shoes and your decisions will be better. Don't just think about your side of the table, he said, but anticipate where conflict can come in.

Early in my career, my bosses discovered that one of my skills was analyzing tax losses and figuring out the rates of return. My accounting class at the University of Vermont had paid off, putting me ahead of the Ivy Leaguers whose curriculum did not include such classes. By age 27, I was put in charge of starting a department for bank clients who were looking for tax shelters, where people could invest their money and get a tax benefit in exchange. I ended up learning a tremendous amount about the oil and gas industry, cattle feeding, movie deals, real estate purchases, and something called the "net lease," which at the time was a small pocket of the real estate world.

The net lease is an investment where the owner of a building leases that building to a tenant but requires that tenant to pay not just rent but also pay the expenses typically associated with ownership, namely the utilities, repairs, taxes, and insurance. This arrangement serves both parties well: the building owner gets the long-term benefits of the investment and a monthly rent payment without having to manage the property, and the tenant gets to use the building as if they own it and can take advantage of the favorable accounting treatment afforded to leases.

Meanwhile, the business can put the capital they would have otherwise invested in owning the building to some other, better use instead. That flexibility is one of the reasons why a net lease is so attractive. But tax laws and regulations can shift the calculation, depending on what is happening in the financial world. It's rarely a great idea for a company to have so much money invested in a fixed asset but selling and then leasing back an asset is a good alternative.

The net lease business did in fact disappear for a few years in the mid-1980s as regulatory changes made the structure impossible. At that time, I shifted into a more conventional real estate role, but after a few years, the environment changed and net leases once again became viable. I was able to use my skills and history to jump right back in. The most important consideration here is that you shouldn't get locked into what you're doing. You may have to adjust as conditions change, and you want to be sure you have the flexibility to move quickly and intelligently. You have to shift as the world shifts around you, just like you do when you're hit with a medical crisis.

This kind of thinking around strategy and risk matters so much in recovery. The very same flexibility that it was important to cultivate in my business life became critical when I was dealing with my health. For all of us, there will be good days and bad days, but knowing how much you should push yourself, and knowing the right amount of risk to take, is so important.

Before I was released from the hospital the first time, doctors encouraged me to consider getting the LVAD device placed in my chest. They warned me that I'd be at terrible risk if I did not. With luck, I had maybe three years of survival without it, but the hope would be for at least ten years or more if I went ahead with the machine. But the price of an LVAD, as I've already said, is a sharply diminished quality of life. You have to wear a heavy battery pack (twelve pounds!) everywhere you go, and there are wires that stick out of your body. At the time, I wasn't ready to make that kind of change to my life. I was convinced I could get myself back to health without it. I knew the risks, but they didn't feel serious enough for me to agree to the procedure.

Truth is, I was also worried about Pam and how the LVAD would affect her life and her role as my partner. We knew there would be sacrifices. We couldn't travel like we had before, and I would be limited. But when faced with certain death otherwise, is there really a choice? When my heart took off in that seriously abnormal rhythm right in front of the doctors, all of a sudden, the landscape shifted. My heart was in the last gasps of being able to function, and the LVAD was the only option to stay alive. Taking that all in was a frightening shock, but I knew what I had to do.

My decision process had to include my wife. We've been together for more than half a century, and I knew she would be supportive. In normal times, the doctor would have introduced us to other LVAD patients, and we could have asked questions and been given a bit of a support system. The restrictions of the coronavirus pandemic made that impossible. A friend of ours knew someone living with an LVAD and Pam was able to arrange a call with his wife. She admits now that it all seemed quite daunting. She would have huge responsibilities for my personal care, from changing bandages every several days to ordering supplies, monitoring my diet, reminding me to take my pills, and generally trying to keep me safe.

There are other impacts. When we travel, we need to figure out which hospitals are within a close distance and familiar enough with the device that we know we can contact them in case of an emergency. I needed to install a generator in my home in case of a power outage and inform the local fire and police departments that electricity is critical to keeping me alive.

All of that said, we've actually almost been surprised at how well we have acclimated to our new normal. Largely it's because I've been able to become stronger and not so dependent on caregivers to function. I wanted to be as independent in my personal life as possible, and that's something else that has driven my recovery.

I remember reading the John O'Hara novel *Appointment in Samarra*, which *TIME* magazine celebrated as one of the top 100 English-language novels written over the past hundred years. In the book, the main character sees the Angel of Death coming for him, and he runs to Samarra to be saved. The problem is that Death knew what would happen, and his plan all along was to meet the man there. That's how I felt in that hospital bed, being told that my heart's ability to function was coming to its end. I wasn't ready to die, so if the LVAD was my best way to cheat death, then it wasn't much of a question as to whether I should go ahead with the procedure.

The doctors opened my chest and installed the device. Fortunately, we were still within the window of opportunity for it to be able to work, where my heart was viable enough to keep going and my physical condition was strong enough to withstand the procedure. Maybe I still wasn't as mentally ready as someone could be, but my lifelong aversion to unnecessary risk made it easy. I wasn't about to play the odds.

Life with an LVAD requires lots of strategic maneuvering, which again plays into the lesson of this chapter. I don't want to be seen as impaired or disabled, especially not in the context of the business world. So I went on a long search for ways to hide the battery pack and wires from view. I tried different types of clothing, shirts, and vests, but none of them felt normal until I found my answer. I stumbled on the website for the athletic clothing manufacturer Under Armour®. The company makes what they call a "football girdle." When worn inside-out, the pockets made to house the football pads are actually a perfect fit for the LVAD batteries. It has become the solution to what was a very frustrating problem.

The other strategic piece is making sure you surround yourself with doctors who actually understand what you're managing. The LVAD, for instance, is not universally known. Not every cardiac patient even ends up with the device as an option because many doctors don't have a great familiarity with it, or any experience with LVAD patients. I had the right doctors and the right hospital. Some people stick with certain doctors or hospitals because they like them, or they're convenient, even if they're not the best for their condition. You can't do that. You can't let personal considerations get in the way of your health. You need to treat it like a business decision and make the smartest choice. My surgeon had performed 1,200 LVAD cases, which is an enormous number. It made my odds of survival so much higher.

In the end, I'm at peace with how the LVAD decision unfolded. Your choices might not have been the same as mine, and that's perfectly reasonable. Understanding the importance of risk doesn't mean that everyone's risk tolerances have to be identical. It just means that you have to be actively thinking about these issues and make decisions that are informed by something real, not just guesswork and blind hope.

We have to be smart about the risks we take, and strategic about the outcomes we are hoping for. While I know I'll never get back to playing basketball like I did in college, and certainly not with the LVAD device inside me, I know my body well enough to have confidence that playing tennis is an achievable goal. We focused early in my recovery on getting me back up on my feet and swinging the racket. We had to. Sports have always brought me so much joy, and the games were such a release from the stresses of the office that I knew that this needed to be a part of my life. The crazy thing is that, as I write this, I'm actually playing tennis better than I ever imagined. My body knows the moves, and the sport has come back to me more quickly than anything else. I spend my court time concentrating on my strokes and have even changed to a two-handed backhand stroke. Thanks to what they call muscle memory, my feet move almost automatically to the right spots.

Getting back into playing shape has motivated me, and it has also defined some of the risks I'm willing to take in my recovery. What's motivating you might be different. You might be willing to take certain risks so that you can travel to see family or see the world.

We all have to define what is most important to us and think about the life we're seeking to live. Just like it's important to find ways to meet my clients' needs despite limitations imposed by the tax laws, we have to find ways to satisfy what motivates us despite our health challenges and the limits we may be facing with our bodies.

I remember running into an issue at work that seemed insurmountable at the time, a potentially industry-killing change in the law that was threatening to derail the whole business. We could have all given up, thrown in the towel, and said we simply need to find another line of work. But it was clear to me that there had to be a solution. There's always a solution, if you're willing to think far enough outside the box. We approached the problem as if it were a puzzle, looking for the unexpected angle, the way to make something work that otherwise seemed impossible. We found it. Our solution was to structure the net lease in a certain way to still make it appealing to business clients. The new structure worked. And that's exactly the same approach to take in your healing. There's going to be a way to get your strength back. There's going to be a way to improve. It may be hard work, it may take time, and it may take exceptional focus, but you can't let yourself give up and think all is lost.

When you're stuck, you can ask yourself: Is there something I'm not doing that I ought to be doing? Is there a way to change tactics to get better faster? It might mean a consultation with a different doctor, it might mean a different set of exercises that you're more motivated to work on, it might mean a new location, or a new schedule, or a different pattern. But we can't just stop strategizing in recovery, or in life. My father gave up, and I firmly believe that it led to his early demise. As long as you are still breathing, there is still hope that you can summon the strength. All is not lost. There is a way.

All of this sets us up perfectly for the next lesson, which is about getting past obstacles. There will always be obstacles in the way, expected and unexpected, and finding the strength to conquer them is critical to recovery. It takes willpower and the right mindset. It takes strength, focus, and the belief that nothing is impossible.

LESSON THREE

When You Hit an Obstacle,
Figure Out a Way Past It

Certainly the economic situation my family faced after my father's death was a huge obstacle that forced me to figure out a path forward, but that's by no means the only time in my life when I've had to come up with a plan. As I discussed in Lesson Two, in my corner of the real estate industry, the world of the net lease, it has been a decades-long battle to stay ahead of the constantly changing laws. It takes not just diligence, but creativity and an insistence on resolving obstacles in order to stay alive.

Of course, this is all even more critical during recovery. You can't just stop at every obstacle and give up. You have to believe you can move past, and then you have to do it, even when it's hard. And it *will* be hard at times. There's no sugarcoating it; life is not always easy. I can believe that there's a silver lining to what happened with my heart, that it has given me more time at home with Pam and more of an appreciation for my kids and grandkids, absolutely. I can talk about how it has given me more gratitude for the good fortune I've had in my life. And, sure, those things are true, but the facts are that this illness has been devastating. It has cut down so many parts of my life. The most apparent is that I am attached to a battery pack, but life is never going to be perfect. We have to make peace with our circumstances, and then set our minds to conquering what we can conquer and making the most of our situations.

I will get through this because I can get through anything. You will get through whatever is standing in your way because you can get through anything too. We all have the same tools, and it's just a matter of how we use them, and how much we train them to serve us. You can do it.

I went into the Army National Guard before the war in Vietnam was at its worst. I was lucky enough to get in under a six-month plan, assigned to Fort Dix, New Jersey. I had been told there was a baseball team there, and in preparation, I spent several weekends at a batting cage in Brooklyn, practicing. For so many years at that point I had only played basketball, so my baseball skills were quite rusty. It didn't take long once I arrived at Fort Dix to realize that Basic Training was not pleasant. Crawling on my hands and knees with bullets being shot just over my head was not for me. I asked permission to try out for the baseball team, not realizing that it required navigating a terrifying chain of command. I was finally able to get a tryout with the caveat that if I failed to make the team, I would find myself on kitchen duty for the rest of my time in the Army. Fortunately, the tryout was a success.

After Basic Training, my next stop was Fort Knox, Kentucky, which was well known at the time for its excellent basketball team. There were three professionals on the team, but I was able to hold my own and I made it through the tryout. We ended up invited to play in an Army tournament. Even better, as my service time was wrapping up and the end of the year approached, the government decided to let everyone with only a month of service remaining go home early for the holidays. My teammates were sad to see me go, but as it turned out, my time serving the country ended up being a lesson in finding a way to navigate a system. Sports became my way past the obstacle of military service, for which I was not particularly well equipped.

When I started my company in 1989, it similarly felt like there were endless roadblocks in my way. I had been doing net leases for over twenty years and, frankly, I was used to success. I had been the youngest vice president ever at Chemical Bank, and I had left a successful company to go out on my own. I had done net leases longer than anyone in the field and had a great track record. Still, getting traction in the marketplace was so hard. My strategy was to approach public pension funds since they had such a clear need for the product. But I learned that pension funds are averse to anything new, and it was impossible to get past the gatekeepers. I had to find new and different ways forward.

It's no different in recovery. My family recounts all of the obstacles I was forced to overcome during my hospitalization. I wasn't even aware of some of them, but one of my colleagues called my hospital stay a "rolling nightmare," my daughter talks about "scare after scare," and my wife has said that it was like the plagues of Passover, one after the next after the next. I had a case of chronic hiccups that would only subside when I slept, exhausting my body. I lost my ability to speak after my vocal cords were damaged from the insertion of the breathing tube when I was first put on a ventilator. The speech therapist in the hospital saw me several times trying to help, and fortunately, my voice finally did return. Then I developed shingles along my right side. They eventually healed, but it was terribly painful in the process. It was one challenge after the next.

When you're an athlete all your life, you understand your body but there are so many things you don't think about until you're incapacitated. To get back the mobility and the stamina you used to have, you need to work on so many different muscle groups. There are muscles that are extremely important that we never think about, all the way down to our toes. I couldn't lift my left foot when I got out of the hospital, so how could I walk? We all think about our biceps and our pectorals, but those aren't always the muscles that are most useful to work on. And often the exercises you need to do in order to make the most progress aren't enjoyable. You would much rather be watching television. But you have to push yourself if you want to get back your strength and function.

My biggest obstacle was the second surgery, getting the LVAD, which set me back almost to the very beginning. The hardest part this time was mental, knowing I'd done all of this already and now had to retrace my steps. There was certainly a lot of frustration. A few weeks earlier there were things I had been able to do, such as hit a tennis ball, walk down a hallway, or lift myself out of bed, and now I could not do those things. My trainers tell me that most people with an LVAD give up many of the things that they used to do. Certainly, they weren't playing sports. It's hard to go anywhere with all the wires and paraphernalia you're forced to carry. You must try to convince yourself that your new, limited life is better than nothing.

But how do you actually do it? How do you move past these obstacles that initially seem impossible to overcome, in life or in recovery? For me, the biggest piece of advice is that so much more of it is mental than you realize. Your body may be standing in your way, but that's why you rely on your doctors and therapists and trainers. They know the exercises you need and the treatments that will give you the best shot. They can help you with the physical piece. But they can't help you find that desire and access that mental strength.

My assistant, Barbara, talks about my willpower to resist even the most tempting bowl of candy on her desk, even when it's something she knows I'd enjoy. But here's the thing: I wouldn't enjoy it knowing that it was something I wasn't supposed to be eating. I wouldn't enjoy it knowing that it was going to keep me from being my best.

Whether it's food, or television, or anything else you might be tempted to overindulge in, you have to focus on the knowledge that in the end, it's not worth it. It's not worth skipping a workout because you'll never get that day back, and you'll be one day behind in your race to recover. If you skip today, what stops you from skipping tomorrow, and the day after that? Pretty soon, you're still in bed, weaker and weaker, and then it's that much harder to start a new streak.

I see such willpower, such mental strength, in the kids who come for programs at the tennis center I built in Vermont. It isn't easy for them to always show up, do their homework, and take part in the activities we provide (which I'll talk more about later in this book). It isn't easy for them to skip hanging out with their friends, and potentially getting in trouble, but they understand that their futures depend on making good choices and building a better life for themselves. So they push through the short-term temptations, and come, day after day, until it's no longer a choice but something they do, and something they love.

We have all seen the stories on television of people born with missing limbs or members of the armed forces returning from battle with challenging injuries. Their strength and determination are inspiring. Matt Stutzman is a medal-winner in archery at the Paralympics and holds the world record for the longest accurate shot. He was born without arms and uses his teeth to string the bow. If that doesn't motivate you, I don't know what would.

I didn't think my own recovery would be as long or as hard as it has been. I've been at it for two years as I write this. I see progress almost every day, but I want so much more. Do I enjoy physical therapy? Not always, but I know it helps, so of course I'm going to do it. It's not even a question. One of my physical therapists met me at my lowest. He thought my condition was so grim that I'd never walk again. But step by step, and day by day, I do it. The magic formula is easy: fight past the excuses. My therapists ask me how I manage to show up every day, no matter how tired. The answer is that I don't give myself a choice not to.

I also put therapy on my schedule. This is an easy trick to getting things done. One of the ways you foster willpower is to make it as simple as possible to do the things you know you should do, and as hard as possible not to. That means that I don't just hope I'll be in the mood to practice my exercises and find some time in my day. I put it in my calendar and treat it as every bit as important as a business meeting. It's even more important, really, because those business meetings aren't going to happen if I'm not strong enough to have them. You need to schedule your life the same way you schedule your work. People wake up on the first Monday of a new month and say they're going to start a new diet or an exercise regimen. They have all the best intentions, all the right goals, but then it usually doesn't stick. They don't treat it like an obligation. They don't put it on paper. They don't set it up in a way that they'll be held accountable.

It's hard to work out by yourself. It's hard to stick to a diet on your own. It's hard to do anything without the kind of support around you (which I'll write about in the next lesson). You can hire trainers or pay for a gym membership if you can afford it, but you can also just ask a friend or family member to help. Instead of doing it alone, you're much more likely to show up if you're meeting someone for a workout. Sometimes the biggest incentive of all is if you're paying someone. Knowing you'll have to pay whether or not you show up makes it that much harder to skip your workout. This doesn't mean you should stretch beyond your means, but it does mean that if getting better is really important to you, then you should find a way to hold yourself accountable for failure.

(Hold your business partners accountable too. In a difficult negotiation, you always want to find a way to make sure the other side suffers a penalty for reneging on a deal or failing to follow through. If you're able to create enough incentive for everyone to push to the finish line, and make it really hard for them to back out, then the deal is far more likely to happen.)

You can't let yourself be overtaken by obstacles. There are always obstacles. You're going to be tired. You're going to feel as if you've used every bit of energy you have. But you have to reach further. You have to have total determination. And if you really don't see a way around an obstacle, you have to keep looking. Go to as many doctors as necessary until you find the one who can improve your condition. Try as many trainers, as many exercises, as many tricks as you can to make those incremental improvements. You have to find the creative answers because they do exist. No one thought there would still be a net lease business by now. No one thought I'd still be alive after what happened to me. But no one should count themselves out. If you feel as if you're falling into a deep despair, just remember—there is a way out. There is always a way out.

In the next lesson, I'll move from overcoming obstacles to surrounding yourself with the right people and fostering the right relationships. Life is all about loyalty and compassion, and the meaningful relationships you build over time are going to be what help power your recovery. Getting better is about smart thinking, for sure, but it's also about a support network, and having the emotional ties to lift you up when things seem bleak and to inspire you to dig even deeper than you can on your own.

LESSON FOUR

Loyalty and Compassion Are the
Keys to Lasting Relationships

People think I'm joking when I tell them I've had the same best friend for over sixty-five years, that I've been married for more than fifty-six years, and that many of the people who work with me have been by my side since the 1970s and '80s. My assistant for the past thirty years still feels like a newcomer to my life.

Relationships are built over time. When there is someone in your life whom you trust and rely on, you can't take that for granted. Those relationships make all the difference in business, in life, and in recovery. So much of why I've been able to have a successful recovery is because there are people by my side who are supporting me. They're looking out for my best interests, they're doing what they can to make things easier for me, and they care. They want me to stick around, and that makes me want to stick around. Without strong, lasting relationships with my family, with my friends, and with my colleagues, I don't know that I'd feel that same push to keep on going.

The lesson of this chapter is about building and maintaining relationships that will bolster you especially when things are at their worst. It's about treating people the way you want to be treated, and assuming the best until evidence forces you to believe otherwise. The advice I first learned from my mentor at Chemical Bank many years ago is that good relationships don't just emerge from luck. They take active management. It's hard to establish bonds and then keep those bonds alive. It takes honesty and compassion, an instinct to treat people fairly, and the ability to give as much of yourself as you can, without expecting anything in return.

I want to start this discussion with some examples from a work context. Running a business gives you so many opportunities to mess up the relationships in your life. People rely on you when you're the boss, and you have to realize that your employees are your responsibility. When I started my own company, I barely slept for three years. It wasn't so much about worry over my own financial risk, since I was confident that, if necessary, I could always find a good job. It was that every two weeks, there were people waiting for me to sign their paychecks. That was a responsibility that kept me awake at night.

This fear drove me to find the path to success. To let these people down, who had trusted me enough to come work for me, would have been extraordinarily painful. You can't ever take someone's trust and loyalty as givens. You have to earn them. You do that by putting yourself in their shoes and thinking about what they need to feel secure, motivated, and happy. In the short-term, maybe this costs you a little bit. You don't have to wait for people to ask for raises or promotions, trying to extract as much value from them as possible. You can see it a different way. You don't want your best employees looking around for other jobs or wondering whether or not you recognize their contributions. You want them to feel respected and comfortable, because that's how you'll keep them for the long run.

Even if it costs you a little more up front, you save so much and your business gains so much from having people there for years. They understand what's going on, don't have to be trained and retrained, and feel invested. You treat people well and make them feel appreciated way before they ever have to ask for something.

It's also the attitude you should have in life. I have to admit that after my freshman year at Vermont, I flirted with the idea of transferring to a school closer to home. New York University was my first choice since their basketball team had a national reputation and seemed to be quite excellent. But I felt uneasy about leaving UVM after they had given me a generous scholarship, treated me so well my freshman year, and truly valued me as a member of the team. As it turned out, the NYU basketball team was rocked with scandal the year I would have transferred in. Multiple players were indicted for their participation in an active gambling ring. Basketball was over at NYU. It would have been a horrendous situation to be involved in, even if I had avoided involvement in the scandal personally. My loyalty to Vermont paid off in ways I couldn't have imagined, but looking back on it now, I'm not that surprised. Loyalty always pays off, and there should never be a question.

I discovered once again how much loyalty pays off when I got sick. For the first time, I couldn't run my business the way I wanted to. For the nearly two months I was in the hospital, it could have been a disaster at work if people had been inclined to take advantage of my situation or if they had been incapable of stepping up and taking charge. But I didn't have to worry because these people who had been with me for decades knew exactly how to proceed, the decisions to make, and the strategies to pursue. It was such a relief to be able to focus on getting better and not wonder if things at work were falling apart. That was more evidence to me of why fostering loyalty over the years and treating people as well as I could were so important.

These very same ideas about how to treat people will help you get the most out of everyone working on your recovery. My trainers have become like family, and I owe so much to them. I also know that they're human beings, motivated by the same forces as everyone else. If you deal with people fairly, respect them, and value them, they will care about you and they will do their very best.

You can't go through a health crisis alone. Or, if you can, you're an extraordinarily unique individual. I certainly can't do it alone. My wife is so absolutely critical to my recovery. She doesn't let me settle. She makes me go for walks, even when I don't want to. She's right there when I'm playing tennis, and even if I don't need her to be standing right there, she's giving me strength, just like she has given me strength for more than fifty years. She's a big reason I'm fighting as hard as I can for more and more days, weeks, months, and years of life. You need to find the people who make you want to fight! For me that's Pam, and, of course, my children and my loving grandchildren. It's also my best friend for the past 65 years, Ronny.

Ronny and I were opponents at first. I met him on the soccer field at age thirteen when our schools were playing each other. I was the goalie, and he didn't like that I blocked his shot. We exchanged words, and he told me to meet him after the game. I didn't want to fight anyone, but I certainly wasn't going to back down. When we met up, well, we realized we'd rather be friends than enemies.

Since I've been sick, I talk to Ronny every day and he has been beyond a friend. He is family. We all need people like Ronny in our lives, people we can be honest with, be completely ourselves, people who know us, flaws and all, and who accept us unconditionally. When I was in the hospital early on in my recovery, it was hard to let most people see or realize my true condition. I didn't want people to perceive me as weak. But you can't keep up a façade forever, and you can't do it with everyone. There have to be people who you're willing to let see you at your worst, who you know won't judge you or change their minds about you. I'm not sure you can really get through a hard situation without them. They are the people who protect you and who shield you from danger.

My assistant, Barbara (the "newcomer"), did such a tremendous job protecting me when I was at my worst. She made sure the office kept running. She kept me updated, brought me any necessary papers, and made it possible for me to still be a part of the team. She says she knew I was getting better when I started to get a little feisty. After three decades she could hear it in my voice.

I've shared the importance of having these relationships, but I want to make sure I also share the way you build them, and the principles you can apply to fostering these kinds of long-term loyalties in your life. You do have to put in effort, and be intentional about it, because these relationships aren't easy. They can vanish if you're not extraordinarily careful.

My first principle is to keep business separate from relationships. It's just like you have to keep your health decisions separate from personal considerations. You never want to compromise your business principles because you're worried about how a choice will play out in your personal life. Just as important, you never want to feel compelled to make personal decisions driven by business. You can work incredibly well with people in a business setting even if you share no personal bond.

My second principle is to always tell people what you think and never let bad feelings linger. This applies equally to personal relationships and business ones. Talk it out, get it all on the table, and find a way to resolve whatever's making you mad. It's not that you have to agree on everything, whether it's in marriage, in friendship, or in business, but you have to listen.

You don't want to hold back, especially since you don't know what the future holds. My daughter, Jen, talks about flying home after my ablation procedure when no one knew if I would ever wake up. She tried to think about the words left unsaid between us, about anything she needed to tell me before I died, anything she wanted me to know, any issues left unresolved, any thoughts left unspoken. She honestly didn't feel like there was anything we'd missed. We talk all the time, we know how we feel about each other, and there are no secrets and no issues bubbling under the surface. That's how it should be. You can't wait for the perfect opportunity to have meaningful conversations. You can't harbor grudges and resentments. You can't keep secrets because you don't know when you might lose your chance to ever reveal them.

This very same principle about directness and honesty definitely applies to the office. You don't want to have lingering disagreements that breed resentment. Honesty, even when it's tough, is so important. People need to know where you stand, and where they stand in your eyes. Be sure people never doubt that you value them. Treat them well and if something is bothering you, tell them. Talk to them and sort it out, whatever the issue is. Make sure people know you're all on the same team.

I met an inspiring woman when I sat on the board of the Women's Sports Foundation. Her name was Rusty Kanokogi, and even though she isn't well-known outside the women's sports world, her story is quite amazing and deserves a much larger audience. She brought women's judo to the Olympic Games (mortgaging her house to pay for the first women's judo world tournament ever, at Madison Square Garden in New York City), and became the team's coach and eventually an inductee into the International Women's Sports Hall of Fame.

But the way she started her career is an amazing story. The only way she was able to compete in judo tournaments was to sign up as a man, and so she did. She disguised herself, cut her hair short, and taped down her breasts. She won her match and went on to win countless others, but when she was outed, she was stripped of all of her medals and honors.

Rusty went on to train in Japan, becoming the first woman to train in the men's group at the Kodokan Judo Institute, the world's judo headquarters. She met her samurai husband there and spent the rest of her life training women in the art of judo. When she was terminally ill with cancer, it was my honor to join her at the Japanese Embassy in New York City where she was awarded the Japanese Medal of Honor, The Order of the Rising Sun. She was also granted the honor of being the only woman interred in the samurai burial plot in Japan.

After Rusty's death, I wanted to do something to ensure her legacy would continue after the life she spent training others. I had told her that I was going to start an endowment in her name to cover travel and training costs for female Olympic hopefuls in judo. She suggested we give the first award to her top student, Kayla Harrison. Rusty passed away in 2009, but she would have been so proud of Kayla, who went on win the 2010 World Judo Championships and then earned gold medals at the 2012 and 2016 Olympic Games.

I'm generally not drawn to the supernatural, and no one would ever call me a touchy-feely kind of guy (except maybe my grandchildren), but I have to confess that in my recovery, I feel Rusty's presence even though she is gone. Once when I was at my sickest, her daughter called with a message she said came directly from Rusty. "Be sure to tell Pam and the family that Richard is not going to die." Somewhere, somehow, Rusty is looking out for me.

In the next lesson, we turn from loyalty to integrity. You can't take shortcuts or behave badly in life. You need to be honest and forthright, and never look for shortcuts that compromise your decency. You need to be able to stand behind all of your actions and go through life being proud of the person you are. Without that, you'll find that when things are tough, the ground might simply crumble beneath you.

LESSON FIVE

Live with Honesty and Integrity

My therapists are shocked when they show up and see that I've actually been practicing between sessions, because many of their patients don't. It makes such a difference and lets one move so much more quickly to the next exercises and the next stages of recovery. It's like being a musician; you won't get better without practice. But while people understand that when it comes to playing the piano, they don't always get it when it comes to physical therapy. They think they'll save all their energy for the session, but it doesn't work that way. There are no shortcuts in recovery or in life. You can't expect to succeed if you don't follow through on commitments and put in the work to get better. You have to be honest with your therapists and with yourself about what you're willing and able to do. You can't lie your way back to full strength. That's what this lesson is about.

Over the course of my career, I've seen many examples of how people's bad behavior can come back to hurt them. Just in the past few years, there was a company in my business space that was expanding so quickly, it would have been only natural to be envious of their growth. They had billions of dollars under management, but it turned out that they were doing deals as quickly as they could. They were not putting in the time to make sure those deals were the right ones, with an acceptable amount of risk. Sure enough, some of them didn't work out, and the company ended up doctoring its financials to hide the reality that they were failing. They got caught, as people do, and now they're out of business.

You have to do the due diligence and make sure your deals are quality. Quality and speed don't always go hand in hand. Just like there are workouts your body needs, even if they take extra effort, they may well be worth it. Eventually you'll see a difference, and if you've only done what's easiest, you will only hurt your own progress in the end.

It does become tempting at times to blame your doctors or trainers if you're not progressing the way you think you should. Usually it's not their fault. It may not be your fault either. Sometimes the body just doesn't do what we want it to do, at least not as quickly as we want it to. Be honest with your doctors about your progress, and about your frustrations. They might have new approaches or different answers. They might not. It might just be that it will take more time. Sometimes that's the only solution.

Most important, you want to foster a relationship where they feel comfortable telling you the truth even if it's not what you want to hear. You don't want them to feel like they have to shade reality to avoid your anger. If you're not working hard enough, you want them to be able to tell you. And if it's just that your goals are impossible to achieve as quickly as you'd like, you want them to tell you that, too, and not give you false hope. It's a balance, for sure, but it all starts and ends with honesty.

I did try to take a shortcut, in a way, when I rejected the LVAD the first time it was offered. I thought I could fix my body without such an extreme intervention, but I couldn't. And once it became clear that I couldn't, I had to be willing to admit that it was time for a different choice. I tell people not to become fixed in their ideas and unable to recognize when situations may have changed. You can't ignore the signs of illness or the indications the body gives off. If there's a reason to investigate a problem, don't wait until it gets worse. Be mindful of catching things early, before they need more significant intervention. I was always on the lookout for cardiac problems because of what happened to my father at a relatively young age, but I was also very healthy, active, and athletic. I'm not sure there was any more I could have done. But you never want to have regrets that you didn't act sooner.

A big part of what drives me to get back to where I was before all of this happened is that I truly love my life. There's nothing I'm hiding from, no conflicts from earlier years that I'm worried will come back to haunt me. It's been very clear to me over time that peace of mind and an acceptance of your choices in life are a big part of remaining happy and content. Money and success alone aren't the keys to the happiest life. There are many things I could have done to make more money.

Don't get me wrong, financial success has absolutely been important to me, especially given how I grew up and what happened to my family after my father's death. But I didn't want to give up knowing my kids and my wife. You see a lot of people in the world who don't act in ways that show that they value time with their families. If all you want is money, you will end up with a lot of sadness. You want to live a life that makes you happy and fulfilled.

Sometimes that's not always clear when you're young. It can be naive for parents to tell their kids to pursue their passions and always enjoy what they're doing. How many of those dreams end up fully realized? You may want to sing, or play or make music, or like me, you might have dreamed of being a professional athlete. Dreams are great, but you may need to test your passions to see if you're good enough to succeed. Just like you need to be honest with the world, you need to be honest with yourself.

You may also want to test some things that may *not* be your passions to see if you can grow to love them. I had no idea when I was young that real estate could become a passion for me, and the basis for an extraordinarily satisfying life. At the same time, tennis might be described as just a hobby, but it's a hobby that has brought me such joy. Just because I wasn't a professional relying on the sport to make a living doesn't mean I haven't been able to strive to compete with the best. I've had amazing opportunities to play with some of the most incredible tennis players in the world, and it's quite likely that I've enjoyed those experiences far more because they were an extra bonus in my life and not what I was counting on to make a living. We underestimate the psychological value of security, sometimes.

My final thought about a life of integrity is that when you feel proud of your actions, and of the person you are, then it's hard to be embarrassed if you need help. I walk pretty well these days, but there are times when I know I'll be safer in a wheelchair or with a cane. You can't let pride get in the way and make you take a risk you don't need to take. Instead, use that feeling of pride to rejoice in yourself and your progress. Dwell in your mind on your accomplishments, not on the areas where you feel like you're struggling. Be proud of what you've been able to do.

In the next lesson, I'll talk about goals, and how crisp, clear, constantly evolving goals are a huge key to making progress in your recovery. Set a goal, reach that goal, and immediately set a new one. You can't become complacent if you want to get back to where you were. You have to push, and setting the right goals gives you specific targets that can motivate you each and every day.

LESSON SIX

Set Goal after Goal after Goal

Not long after leaving the hospital after the first crisis, I set a goal for myself. I was going to a U.S. Open dinner in a few months, and I wanted to walk in under my own power, and not be in a wheelchair. No one thought it would ever happen, not my doctors, not my trainers, and I'm not even sure my family thought I could do it. But that goal drove me, day after day, and pushed me forward. As the event approached, I could feel myself getting stronger and stronger, knowing that victory was within my reach. That morning, I grabbed a cane and I walked into that dinner on my own two feet, without assistance.

I suppose I could have stopped there, satisfied with my progress, and proud to have done what I set my mind to. Of course, I didn't stop. I set another goal, and when I met that one, it was full speed ahead to the next, and the next after that. I'm always setting goals because that's how I drive progress. I ask myself what is possible next that isn't possible now. What will motivate me to push harder, get better, and recover more quickly?

It's the same way that I've always approached my business life, my philanthropic work, and my personal pursuits such as tennis. How many new transactions can I close? Who am I in a unique position to help? What will make me proud to have accomplished and motivate me every day to push myself to my limits?

To me, success in life is all about goal setting, especially in recovery. You have to look forward and know what you're aiming for in order to ever get there. You have to have a reward in mind, a target, and a vision of your future. Then you have to do everything in your power to achieve that vision. That's how you reach new heights.

My whole life has been goal after goal. There is nothing I've done for which I didn't set a goal. When I was playing high school basketball, I was watching friends of mine who I knew weren't as good as I was, yet they were making the all-prep team, recognized by the newspaper. They were playing at bigger schools and the papers were paying more attention, but that didn't mean I couldn't find a way to be recognized too. I talked to my coach and told him he had to contact the newspaper and let them do whatever they do so our team could get noticed. He listened to me, and I ended up making honorable mention one year, and then the all-prep second team the following season. I wanted to get on the team because I knew it would be important in helping me reach my next goal; I needed to earn a scholarship to college. And college was going to be the necessary step to the goal after that, overcoming what happened to my father and becoming financially stable.

I still remember the moment I felt like I reached some level of financial stability. Back at that time, you needed a $10,000 annual salary to get an American Express card. When I started at the bank, I was making $5,200 plus a $500 bonus. So it took a few years. But I finally did reach a $10,000 salary, I was able to get the card, and then I was off and running to the next goal.

I was driven by the desire to get as good as I could at tennis, play in the Maccabiah Games, and eventually to build my own company from scratch. These were all goals that motivated me.

Every goal has obstacles along the way. There is always frustration when you don't think you'll get there, but that's when you have to dig in and really push yourself. If it's too easy, it's the wrong goal, and you have to move the goalpost. There's no point in challenging yourself to do something easy. That's not how you grow. It has to be hard.

Of course, your goals also have to be realistic, and they have to be things that you feel confident will make you happy when you reach them. You may set a goal and then find out when you really dedicate yourself to it that it's not quite what you thought it would be. Maybe it doesn't make you as happy as you imagined, or the obstacles are just too great to overcome. While you can't let bumps get in the way, you also can't be silly about it. If my goal had been to become a professional ballplayer, I suspect that just wasn't going to be realistic, I would have kept bumping up against impossible obstacles, and if I hadn't changed the goal at some point, I would have been setting myself up for a life of disappointment.

You see, there's a difference between a goal and a wish. You can fill a wish list with all kinds of dreams, all kinds of reaches that may or may not actually come true. Working out every single day of the year, perhaps, or something more aspirational, such as winning a marathon. Wish list items aren't necessarily within your control. You can try to work out every day, but you also have to understand that something, whether illness or other obligation, might end up getting in your way. And you can train to win a marathon but there might always be someone faster than you, and you can't really control that.

Making sure goals are within your control is really important. When I started my company, I thought it would be easier to find clients then it was. I've already mentioned how pension funds were far more resistant to new products than I expected them to be, but this wasn't the only hurdle. We had one client who had been giving us a great deal of business, more business than we could ever handle, honestly. We thought it was going to be our way to stay successful forever, but then the business was sold, as often happens, and the new buyers weren't interested in net leases. They wanted international real estate instead. So we found new customers, and a similar thing happened. It could never have been a true goal to find one company to meet all of our needs because that was out of our control. We couldn't prevent a customer from being sold to new owners who had other ideas in mind. We also couldn't control the broader economy, such as when the financial crisis hit in 2008. If our goals had been dependent on the world being predictable and unchanging, we would have hit hurdle after hurdle. You have to choose goals that you have the power to achieve, without relying on external factors that you will never be able to control.

It frightens me to look back at my recovery sometimes and think about those early goals and just how debilitated I really was. I tried not to focus on what others were saying about my recovery at the beginning, but I know that there were people who thought I'd never walk again. Certainly no one imagined I would be hitting a tennis ball. I couldn't dwell on those people, though. There are always going to be people who distract you from your goals, who try to bring you down and make you see the negative side of your situation. You have to ignore them and avoid them when possible. You want people who are lifting you up toward the goals, and not keeping you from them.

In a way, that's a big difference between a good trainer and a *great* trainer. My trainers see my limitations, of course, but they don't linger on them. They believe in me, and they see that I'll do the work so they set goals for me too. I want them to set goals for me. I want them to have outcomes we're working together to reach, and I want them to feel pride when I reach them. You need those kinds of trainers in your recovery, the ones who aren't just clocking in for an hour and then leaving, not thinking about you between sessions or caring about your overall progress. You need people invested in your recovery, rooting for you, and putting the pieces in place to help you reach those unreachable goals that you have in mind.

My trainers talk about the importance of goals and of markers and milestones along the way. You can set as many milestones as you want, one of my trainers has said, but if the patient isn't determined to reach them, nothing else matters. It doesn't matter what the trainer does, what the family does, or what the doctor does. It is all about the patient's desire and determination. There are people who express desire but then don't follow through. They let things distract them, whether phone calls during training sessions or scheduling conflicts that they don't bother to fix. They don't work out between sessions. They don't push themselves. They don't have the hunger to improve.

I take videos every time I hit a tennis ball because I want the trainers to see, and I want to watch the videos myself. I want to see where my weaknesses and strengths are. I want to make sure I'm not overestimating or underestimating my progress. I want as much information as I can gather, to make adjustments and keep improving. I want as much data as I can get, just like I want in the business context. I want to know my heart rate, my blood pressure, all of those numbers, because I want to be able to see what's going on inside my body and stay on course toward my goals.

If this sounds like a lot of effort and energy to put toward recovery, you're right. But no one said it should be easy. Success in any realm, business or otherwise, is never easy. Setting goal after goal isn't the recipe for an easy, carefree, relaxing existence. It's a recipe for hard work, but it's also a recipe for success. If it's too easy, you're not working hard enough. You need to increase your goals, become more ambitious, and push harder. If you can't see progress, and you don't really sense how far you've come, you probably haven't gone far enough.

But what gives you that hunger and drive to keep pushing? I've talked about family and friends, but for most of us, it's more than that. We need things we care about in life, areas where we feel like we're making a difference and helping the world become a better place, whether in big ways or small. The next lesson is about that bigger picture, those things that drive us and keep us going. It's about the things we're working for in the world, the ways we're contributing and giving back. It's about the ultimate goal for all of our lives: to leave the world a better place for generations to come. That's where I turn next.

LESSON SEVEN

Give Back, Whenever You Can

My family ended up with almost nothing after my father died, but we survived because of the generosity of others. Without my scholarships or without the relative who sent me small checks in the mail, it's not clear where I'd be. I take my responsibility to give back very seriously, and the truth is that there's no greater reward than being able to use my success to help people who need a hand.

I fell in love with Vermont during college, and my family returned there many times over the years. Eventually we bought a weekend house in Bennington and started to get involved in the community. My first thought was to build a tennis center, for obvious and perhaps selfish reasons, as I really wanted to have a nice place to play. As I thought more about it, I realized that the real reason to do it was to help the town, especially the underserved population of kids who could use a helping hand. Bennington is a small, working-class town, suffering from all of the plagues of a big city, with poverty and unemployment.

I saw a need for lots of kids to have a place to go after school, a safe place, offering a meal and some help with their homework. And I had a vision of where tennis could fit into that plan. I imagined that if they could learn the sport, some of them might come to feel the same way I do when executing a great serve or a long volley back and forth, that thrill of competition and the fun of the game. Most of the kids in the community had never even picked up a tennis racket; tennis was seen as a sport for rich people. But it was clear that a program combining tennis instruction with mentoring, food, and support could really help many kids and their families.

I always had a desire to help develop young tennis players, but the program in Vermont became so much more than that. It wasn't just about tennis, but about giving many kids in the area who needed assistance something to help them stay off the street. I worked with the U.S. Tennis Association Foundation to give these kids an activity they could get involved in, and to incor- porate an educational piece, afterschool tutoring, and free meals and supplies. Remembering how it felt not to be able to afford that baseball glove my freshman year of college, everything we do is free. The programs and camps cost the kids and their families nothing, and we give the kids a tennis racket and sneakers at no charge.

One of the hardest parts of the plan was convincing local school principals that tennis wasn't just an activity for the wealthy, but a sport that could benefit anyone, and one that kids could learn quickly. Initially, the first principal we met with was very resistant. He said, "I've crossed three sports off of my list: tennis, golf, and skiing." He thought of them as elite sports. But after we made the presentation, he was all in. He said, "This is the best thing I've ever seen." He now provides us with as many children as he can to participate in our program after school. He helped bring on three other schools as well. We redesigned the tennis bubble to include one smaller court and two classrooms.

We worked very hard to figure out how to get kids hooked on the game and then to design a sustainable program that could grow over time. I had to hire the right people to help fit together all the pieces and be personally involved and invested to make sure it was successful. Eventually we grew and succeeded to the point that our chapter of the National Junior Tennis and Learning networks, one of 250 sites across the country, is now held up as one of the most successful and most dedicated to helping underserved children.

We've gotten amazing feedback over the years. The program has impacted hundreds of kids, and in addition to the tennis and the tutoring, we get them out in the community in ways they don't normally experience. We've taken them to museums, to Albany, and to all kinds of cultural destinations. One time, on a trip to a museum in Albany, one child thought we were actually in New York City, and he was shocked to find out we weren't. He had never seen tall buildings before, and just assumed we were in the Big Apple.

The kids in the program are largely kids who live below the poverty line, who've never been outside of Bennington, Vermont, and we've tried to open up new worlds for them. It's spectacular to see these kids, who've never heard of tennis, getting really good and even pursue the sport on the high school level. We also run summer programs with all the bells and whistles, and we provide a free backpack full of school supplies to ready these kids for the start of school in the fall.

My involvement in philanthropic efforts around kids and tennis actually started with an amazing friendship I developed with the tennis legend Billie Jean King. She and I met because I had become known in Manhattan as someone in the city who could play well, and who was available to practice with tennis pros. There are very few places to play tennis in the city, and very few people available to hit during the day.

Billie and I became good friends, and eventually she told me about her work with the Women's Sports Foundation. She invited me to join the board of directors, which was a wonderful experience. That was how

I met Rusty Kanokogi. There were Olympic medalists on the board, tremendous athletes, and it was a thrill to be involved. At one point, the University of Vermont knew of my connection to Billie, and they asked me to see if she would be willing to give the school's commencement address. She knocked it out of the park, giving a wonderful speech with three pieces of advice that fit nicely with the themes of this book: learn how to learn, relationships are everything, and be a problem solver. Relationships are absolutely everything, as I've discussed, and solving problems is the most important thing we have to do. As far as learning how to learn, it's all about having strategic insights, and the way you get them is by absorbing as much knowledge as you possibly can across all areas.

Billie changed the way I saw the world and gave me the opportunity to make an impact. When I played tennis with her, people would constantly come up to her and tell her that she changed their life. She used her platform as a celebrity to advocate for gender equality and other issues important to her, and it showed me how someone can strive to contribute and really make a difference. Of course, I'm not a celebrity like she is, but I do have the ability to give to causes that matter, and her example showed me how I can make the most of that chance, especially through my work with youth tennis.

A few years ago, I was beyond honored to receive the U.S. Tennis Association Foundation's annual "Serving Up Dreams" award for my work on the tennis program. There really are very few things you can do in life to have such a dramatic impact on people, and kids in particular. I am so lucky to have found a hands-on, real time opportunity to help children become better citizens and better people and help the parents who so desperately want their children to succeed but who maybe aren't in the position to give them a program like this.

It makes me so proud that the hard work I've done in my career put me in the position to give back in this way, but I also look back in amazement because if you'd told me any of this as a kid, it wouldn't have even made sense. I didn't know anything about charitable giving. I was a recipient, not a donor, but I know how much impact it all had on me, so I've always felt that I have to give back.

When I first saw the people around me in business doing charitable work, I could tell that some of it was for their egos. They wanted their names on things, and to be able to tell other people about the good work they were doing. I didn't get that. Instead, I craved the good feeling you get when you help someone. Of course, you can have that at every level. There are so many things each of us can do that show we care, no matter our means. Whenever my grandmother received a flyer requesting a donation, she used to send $5. For her and her budget, it was a meaningful amount, and knowing she did that made an impact on me growing up. Whether it was from the Red Cross or UJA or the March of Dimes, she responded. I sometimes think about the fact that there are more than two hundred million adults in the United States. If 10 percent of them gave $5 to charity, that's over $100 million. Just imagine the collective impact of that money. It could do wonders. And, of course, if you can't give money, give time. There are always ways to help.

Perhaps one of the unexpected things about my illness is that it has made me look outward even more than inward and think about more people I can help in the time I have left. When I was in the hospital, I saw people suffering in so many different ways and was exposed to people beyond the business circles I'd been stuck in for years. I started to think about new ways to contribute, and the amazing thing about focusing on other people's problems is that it helps to take your mind off your own suffering. It's easy in recovery to get bogged down in your own challenges and forget that others have walked these paths, and paths even more trying than yours.

You are not alone, in triumph or in pain. Others know how you are feeling.

Youth tennis is not the only cause with which I've become involved over the years. I've looked for areas where I can actually get personally involved and make a difference with the unique skills and interests that I'm able to bring to the table. I've given to the University of Vermont for obvious reasons, to pay them back for taking a chance on me. I started a fellowship in the Holocaust Studies program there and have given to hospitals to help doctors fund their research. Many nonprofits would love to have more people with business experience come and help; they often need that expertise. So when I find ways to be valuable, I like that.

The best opportunities to give back come from places where you have a personal connection and can actually be useful in a specific and meaningful way. After my heart surgery, I was so grateful to the doctor who performed the procedure. I asked him how I could help more people benefit from these amazing medical advances. I set up a fund to endow a fellowship to train more doctors to perform these kinds of life-saving surgeries. It's certainly helpful to give money to large organizations, even when you don't know what that money will be directly used for, but it's even better to find ways to contribute, whether with money, time, or expertise, in ways where you can see the results first-hand and know that your contribution mattered.

I think this is a good place to note again how lucky we are to benefit from the wonders of modern medicine. So many good people, including my father, were lost far too soon because we hadn't yet learned all there is to know about healing and the body. It's just remarkable what doctors can do these days.

My charitable work is a big part of what keeps me motivated to recover. I want to see these projects through, watch them grow and help more and more people, and continue to be involved. I'm invested in the success of everything I contribute to and can't bear to think about not being around to see what we can accomplish. I insist on weekly calls about my tennis program and regular updates on everything else I'm involved in. You need to stay engaged and active in everything you do, and keep contributing, as much as you can. I want to see my business succeed, and I want to see these efforts succeed and see people's lives changed. It's a big piece of what keeps me going.

This relates in a lot of ways to why I wanted to write this book. I ask myself what the highest use of my time is, and I know that there are people going through these same kinds of difficulties, needing the same kind of hope as I've needed at times along the way. There are many people whom I've mentored over the years, giving advice to help them launch their careers, but who's there to fill that same function when you get sick? Who do people have to turn to when they need that motivation to recover and get better, to stay positive and know that they can't give up? That's what I hope people can take from this book, to see that there are others out there who've been down this road and emerged with strength. I hope people can see that you don't have to be defined by your limitations, but you can stretch beyond them, and keep living your life and making a difference. So much of recovery keeps you in a bubble, thinking only about your own body and your own pain, but you can still try to shift your focus outside, keep giving back, and creating meaning in the world.

The last lesson I want to share is about never accepting limits. I know there are many people, especially in the hospital, who looked at me and thought, *What's the tragedy here? This is a man in his late 70s; what can he expect?* I don't accept that and neither should you (whether you're older than me or younger). And I especially have no interest in adopting that mindset myself. You are only as old as you behave. And you are never too old to recover and come back from illness and injury. As long as you're still breathing, you can get stronger and improve your circumstances.

LESSON EIGHT

*You're Never Too Young, and
You're Never Too Old*

Many people dismissed the odds of my recovery just because I'm nearly eighty years old. *He's had his life*, they think. *He's done.* But in a lot of ways, you're only as old as you feel. As long as you have your mental capacity, you can be just as productive as you were when you were younger. I've spent a lifetime taking care of my body, playing sports, and staying fit, and this is when that work pays off. My athletic background put me in a position to be able to recover from this, and there's no reason to accept anything less.

At the same time, we often underestimate young people too. We think they lack gravitas or wisdom, when that's not necessarily the case. The young people in my office are some of the most talented, the hungriest, and the ones most willing to think outside the box. Your age really doesn't matter. We are all able to reach new heights and can all perform at our peak. And yet at the same time, we are all tempted to sometimes make excuses, and tell ourselves it's okay to underperform simply because we're old, or tired, or young, or inexperienced, or any of countless ideas we can talk ourselves into. They're excuses, all of them, and they serve as limits on what we can accomplish. We can't accept limits. We need to push past them and rise above.

Would it be silly to say that before my illness, I never really thought about chronological age? As far as I was concerned, I was still twenty-five. Of course, my tennis game wasn't as fast or agile as it had been a few decades ago, but I was still effective on the court and able to hold my own. People told me I looked younger than my age, which was one of the reasons I had started playing tennis in the first place, seeing how young the players looked. It was surprising to me that over the years I saw many of my tennis partners quit the sport and move to golf. Golf is easier, but once you start to take it easy, your body falls apart. Tennis is a great workout. There's hand-eye coordination, cardio, stops and starts, strength, and flexibility. There are people playing tennis into their 80s and

90s, and I think it's terrific. Golf is a lot of walking and standing still. And if you use a cart, it's really not much exercise at all, not a lot of activity. We expect to see older people playing golf. But older people playing tennis? I think we have an expectation people should slow down. It's a silly expectation, and there's no reason to feed into it if you're still able to function.

In the office, I found it incredibly frustrating if people thought someone in his 70s shouldn't be running things. You can be at the top of your game, with all of those years of experience only serving to help you make smarter and better decisions, buttressed with hard-earned evidence and wisdom. We were doing deals that were expected to last seven to ten years and investors had started asking about my succession plan. I was happy to have one, but I also felt like it was disrespectful. I was doing just fine. I look at people who retire in their 60s and it confuses me. Once you retire, your mind can get old really quickly. Without much to occupy you, all you can do is fall apart. You want to stay active, physically and mentally, for as long as you can.

Frankly, I think the lack of older people still engaged in the workforce is a real shame. When you're not the boss, I know it can be hard. People are afraid to hire older workers, partly because they can be more expensive given their years of experience, and partly because society sees them as in decline. I would love to see more people in their 80s and 90s still active in business, and I think a lot of them could handle it.

In many ways, I think staying young is about attitude. You can't get stuck in old habits and think you know better. You need to stay in tune with what younger people are doing because that keeps you evolving. My assistant jokes that I spend too much time staring at my smartphone, just like kids these days, but I take it as a compliment. She thinks I'm too available, doing work at nine at night instead of sticking to the old 9-to-5 routine people had when I was growing up. But I know the world has changed. Expectations have changed, and business has changed. Why shouldn't I be experiencing the same reality as younger people are? Why is it assumed that someone my age can't figure out how to use a computer?

I learn from the young people in my life just as much as I expect them to learn from me. We were thrilled to hire people in their 20s at my company, and I'm excited to see what their approach to the business is, and how it may be different from mine. There are always new things to learn. (And I hope they feel the same way, because my generation also has lots of things to teach.) You don't just want to spend time with people your age. You want to broaden your horizons.

It's easy to be satisfied with second best. It's easy to be satisfied with mediocrity. It's easy to be satisfied with sixty, sixty-five, seventy, or even seventy-five years of productive life. But you can't. You can be proud of what you've accomplished but still know that there can be more left, much more. You can't give up. If you embark on something thinking that you won't be able to do it, you'll probably fail. You need to think you're going to succeed, and in fact you need to know you're going to succeed. You need to have confidence in yourself for you to expect anyone else to have any confidence in you.

What drives me now is the same thing as what would have driven me had this all happened thirty or forty years ago. I have work left undone. I have relationships I care about and people I love and want to keep getting to spend time with. I have deals I want to do, and business I want to win. I have tennis matches to play, grandkids to enjoy, causes to champion, and people to help. I have strategies to formulate, obstacles to work my way past, and goals to achieve. All kinds of goals, I promise.

And here's the thing: *you* have all of that too. I know you do. We all do. We have all been put on this planet to achieve amazing things with our lives, and illness shouldn't derail us completely. We can all summon the strength to keep fighting, summon the power to keep trying, and summon the desire to be the best we can be. We can all improve, we can all overcome, we can all rally. I hope my story and my lessons have helped inspire you, and I wish you all the strength in the world as you push yourself back to old heights and onto new ones.

If I could do it, so can you.

I promise!